TAS-HEELUT TAA-REEKH

1

Tasheel-ul-Taareekh Level 1
First Impression 2004
Second Impression 2008

Jamiatul Ulama Taalimi Board:
Curriculum Development Committee

1st Floor, Baitul Hamd,
32 Dolly Rathebe Road,
Fordsburg 2092,
South Africa
E-mail: taalimi@islamsa.org.za

As with any educational material, the contributors have been influenced by a number of people to whom they have spoken and books they have read. The contributors acknowledge this with appreciation.

The Curriculum Development Committee have made every effort to ensure accuracy.

A copy of the British Library Cataloguing-in-Publication Data is available from the British Library.

ISBN: 1-919942-03-3

Design: Stratford Design UK

Contents

Bismillahir Rahmaanir Raheem بسم الله الرحمن الرحيم

INTRODUCTION TO *HISTORY*

Allaah ﷻ has revealed the Qur'aan as the final guide to mankind. The Qur'aan contains various commands relating to worship, monetary dealings, and social conduct, as well as stories of the people of the past. The Qur'aan informs us of the mission of the Prophets of Allaah ﷻ and how communities responded to the call of the Prophets عليهم السلام.

The purpose of these stories is to teach mankind how mighty nations were destroyed, how truth always prevails over falsehood, and how we can learn from the history of previous generations. Allaah ﷻ says:

"Verily there is a lesson for people of intelligence in their stories"

(Surah Yoosuf, Juz 13)

History enables us to learn from the past. It gives us the opportunity to change our present circumstances and empowers us to plan for the future. It serves to strengthen our faith in the mercy of Allah ﷻ, and as a reminder of how the wrath of Allah ﷻ, destroys sinners.

Lesson one

Aadam عَلَيْهِ السَّلَامْ

1. Aadam عَلَيْهِ السَّلَامْ was the first man created by Allaah تَعَالى.
2. Allaah تَعَالى created Aadam عَلَيْهِ السَّلَامْ from clay
3. Allaah تَعَالى taught Aadam عَلَيْهِ السَّلَامْ the names and benefits of all things in nature.
4. Allaah تَعَالى commanded the angels to make sajdah to Aadam عَلَيْهِ السَّلَامْ.
5. Shaytaan did not obey the command of Allaah تَعَالى.
6. He refused to make sajdah to Aadam عَلَيْهِ السَّلَامْ.
7. Hawwaa رَضِيَ اللّٰهُ عَنْهَا was the wife of Aadam عَلَيْهِ السَّلَامْ.
8. She was created from the left rib of Aadam عَلَيْهِ السَّلَامْ.
9. Aadam عَلَيْهِ السَّلَامْ and his wife Hawwaa رَضِيَ اللّٰهُ عَنْهَا lived for a long time in jannah.

Keywords:

Aadam	created	rib
Hawwaa	command	

Questions

1. Who was the first man created by Allaah تَعَالَى?

2. What was Aadam عَلَيْهِ السَّلَامْ wife's name?

3. Where did Aadam عَلَيْهِ السَّلَامْ and Haw'wah رَضِيَ اللّٰهُ عَنْهَا live?

4. What did Allaah تَعَالَى command the angels to do?

5. Did shaytaan obey the command of Allaah تَعَالَى?

Lesson one

Aadam عَلَيْهِ السَّلَامْ

Aadam

Hawwaa

rib

Colour in activity

Hawwa
rib
created
command

Lesson two

Aadam عَلَيْهِ السَّلَامْ on Earth

1. Aadam عليْهِ السَّلَامْ stayed with his wife Hawwaa عَلَيْهِ السَّلَامْ in jannah.
2. Allaah تعَالى told them that they could eat from all the trees of jannah except one tree.
3. Shaytaan tricked them into eating from the tree.
4. They begged for Allaah's تعَالى forgiveness.
5. Allaah تعَالى forgave them for their mistake but they could no longer live in jannah
6. Allaah تعَالى sent them to stay on earth. He also sent Shaytaan to earth.
7. Aadam عَلَيْه السَّلَامْ was the first man and the first Nabee of Allaah تعَالى.
8. A Nabee is sent to earth to guide people to the straight path.

Keywords:

jannah	forgave	tricked
Shaytaan	earth	

Questions

1. What did Allaah تعالى tell them to do?

2. Who tricked them?

3. Did Allaah تعالى forgive them for their mistake?

4. Who was the first man and first Nabee of Allaah تعالى?

5. Who did Allaah تعالى send as a Nabee to earth?

Lesson two

Aadam عَلَيْهِ السَّلَامْ on earth

jannah

forgave

آدَم

Colour in activity

jannah

tricked

shaytaan

forgave

earth

Lesson three

Nooh عَلَيْهِ السَّلَامْ

1. The people of Nooh عَلَيْهِ السَّلَامْ worshipped idols of their elders who had passed away.
2. His people were sinful, unjust and cruel.
3. Nooh عَلَيْهِ السَّلَامْ invited his people for 950 years to the worship of Allaah تَعَالى.
4. The humble people obeyed his teachings.
5. The proud people called him a liar and continued to worship their idols.
6. His wife and son also refused to accept his teachings.
7. Those who called him a liar, made fun of him and told him to bring down the punishment of Allaah تَعَالى if he was a true Nabee.
8. After inviting them for 950 years, Nooh عَلَيْهِ السَّلَامْ asked Allaah تَعَالى to punish them.

Keywords:

elders	proud
invited	punish

Questions

a. What did the people of Nooh عَلَيْهِ السَّلَامْ worship?

....

b. What did Nooh عَلَيْهِ السَّلَامْ do for 950 years?

....

c. Who obeyed Nooh عَلَيْهِ السَّلَامْ?

....

d. What did the proud people do?

....

e. Did his son and wife accept his teachings?

Lesson three

Nooh عَلَيْهِ السَّلَامْ

Nooh

proud

punish

Colour in activity

elders

invited

proud

punish

Lesson four

The building of the ark

1. Allaah تعالى accepted the du'a of Nooh عَلَيْهِ السَّلَامْ and told him to build an ark.
2. People laughed at Nooh عَلَيْهِ السَّلَامْ and his followers while they were building the ark.
3. When the ark was ready Allaah تعالى ordered Nooh عَلَيْهِ السَّلَامْ to place a pair of every living creature, a male and female in the ship.
4. 82 people who believed in his message joined him on the ark. His wife and son refused to board the ark.
5. Allaah تعالى brought about a great flood.
6. All living things drowned in this flood.
7. Only Nooh عليهِ السَّلَامْ and his people on the ship were saved.

Keywords:

ark	drowned
flood	saved

Questions

a. What did Allaah تَعَالَى order Nooh عَلَيْهِ السَّلَامْ to do?

....

b. What did the people do to Nooh عَلَيْهِ السَّلَامْ and his followers? ....

c. Explain what happened when the ark was ready?

....

d. What were the results of the flood?

....

e. Who was saved from the flood?

....

Lesson four

The building of the ark

ark

flood

saved

Colour in activity

ark

flood

drowned

saved

Lesson five

Ibraaheem عَلَيْهِ السَّلَامْ

1. People worshipped idols during the time of Ibraaheem عَلَيْهِ السَّلَامْ
2. Ibraaheem عَلَيْهِ السَّلَامْ father's name was Aazar. Aazar made and sold idols.
3. People also prayed to the stars, the moon, and the sun.
4. Ibraaheem عَلَيْهِ السَّلَامْ only worshipped one Allaah.
5. One day he broke all the idols in the temple.
6. Ibraaheem عَلَيْهِ السَّلَامْ was brought before Namrood, the king of the people.
7. The king threw Ibraaheem عَلَيْهِ السَّلَامْ into a huge fire.
8. Allaah تعالى ordered the fire to become cool and safe for Ibraaheem

Keywords:

Ibraaheem	idols
worshipped	temple

Questions

a. What did the people worship during the time of Ibraaheem عَلَيْهِ السَّلَامْ? ....

b. Name the father of Ibraaheem عَلَيْهِ السَّلَامْ.

....

c. What did Ibraaheem's عَلَيْهِ السَّلَامْ father do for a living?

....

d. Besides the idols, what else did the people pray to?

....

e. What did the king do to Ibraaheem عَلَيْهِ السَّلَامْ?

....

Lesson five

Ibrahim عَلَيْهِ السَّلَامْ : Idol worshipping

Ibraheem

idols

إِبْرَاهِيم

Colour in activity

Ibraaheem

idols

worshipped

temple

Lesson six

The sacrifice of Ibraaheem عَلَيْهِ السَّلَامْ

1. Ibraaheem عَلَيْهِ السَّلَامْ was 86 years old, when his son Ismaaeel عَلَيْهِ السَّلَامْ was born.
2. When Ismaaeel عَلَيْهِ السَّلَامْ was born, his father left him and his mother Haajirah رَضِيَ اللّٰهُ عَنْهَا in the valley of Makkah.
3. Makkah was a desert with no people and no houses
4. Ismaaeel عَلَيْهِ السَّلَامْ grew up as a strong boy who later helped his father.
5. Allaah تَعَالَى ordered Ibraaheem عَلَيْهِ السَّلَامْ to sacrifice his son Ismaa'eel عَلَيْهِ السَّلَامْ.
6. Ibraaheem عَلَيْهِ السَّلَامْ told his son about the command of Allaah تَعَالَى.
7. Ismaaeel عَلَيْهِ السَّلَامْ replied: *"O' my beloved father! do as you are commanded. You will `Inshaa Allaah' find me from among the patient."*
8. Allaah تَعَالَى saved Ismaaeel عَلَيْهِ السَّلَامْ and sent a ram to be slaughtered in his place.

Keywords:

kaabah	Eedul-adhaa	Ismaaeel
ram	makkah	Haajirah

9. During Eedul-Adhaa we slaughter an animal to remember the sacrifices of Ibraaheem عليهِ السّلَامْ and Ismaaeel عليهِ السّلَامْ
10. Ibraaheem عَلَيْهِ السَّلَامْ and Isma'eel عَلَيْهِ السَّلَامْ later built the ka'bah in Makkah.

Questions

a. How old was Ibraaheem عَلَيْهِ السَّلَامْ when his son Isma'eel عَلَيْهِ السَّلَامْ was born? ....

b. Where did Ibraaheem عليهِ السّلَامْ leave Ismaaeel عليهِ السّلَامْ and Haajirah رَضِيَ اللّٰهُ عَنْهَا ....

c. Where were Ismaaeel عليهِ السَّلَامْ and his mother left?

....

d. What did Allaah تَعَالَى order Ibraaheem عَلَيْهِ السَّلَامْ to do?

....

e. What did Allaah تَعَالَى do?

....

Lesson six

Ibrahim عَلَيْهِ السَّلَامْ : Family life

Kaabah

Eedul-adha

كَعْبَة

Colour in activity

Kaabah

Eedul-adha

ram

Makkah

Ismaeel

Haajirah

Lesson seven

Yoosuf عَلَيْهِ السَّلَامْ

1. Yaaqoob عَلَيْهِ السَّلَامْ had twelve sons. Yoosuf عَلَيْهِ السَّلَامْ was his most loved son.
2. Yoosuf عَلَيْهِ السَّلَامْ was very handsome, pious and clever.
3. His brothers were jealous of him because Yaaqoob عَلَيْهِ السَّلَامْ loved him very much.
4. His brothers threw him into a well to get rid of him.
5. Some travellers found him in the well and sold him as a slave in Egypt.
6. He was bought by a master who treated him as his own son.
7. His master's wife falsely blamed him of doing wrong and sent him to jail.
8. Yoosuf عَلَيْهِ السَّلَامْ was respected by the other prisoners because he was pious and kind.

Keywords:

Yaaqoob	slave	threw
well	Yoosuf	pious

Questions

a. How many sons did Yaaqoob عَلَيْهِ السَّلَامْ have?

....

b. Why were the brothers of Yoosuf عَلَيْهِ السَّلَامْ jealous of him? ....

c. What did his jealous brothers do?

....

d. Why was Yoosuf عَلَيْهِ السَّلَامْ put into jail?

....

e. Why was Yoosuf عليْهِ السَّلَامْ respected in jail?

....

Lesson seven

Yoosuf عَلَيْهِ السّلامْ: Idol worshipping

Yoosuf

pious

يوسف

Colour in activity

Yaqoob

well

slave

Yoosuf

threw

pious

Lesson eight

Yoosuf عَلَيْهِ السَّلَامْ in Egypt

1. Yoosuf عليْهِ السَّلَامْ was well known for giving the meaning of dreams.
2. The king had seen a dream and called Yoosuf عليْهِ السَّلَامْ to give the meaning of his dream.
3. The king freed Yoosuf عَلَيْهِ السَّلَامْ from jail and made him a minister.
4. There was a drought and no food in Egypt.
5. Yoosuf عَلَيْهِ السَّلَامْ brothers came from their country to Egypt in search of food.
6. They did not know who the minister was. He treated them kindly and gave them food.
7. He later forgave his brothers for the wrong they had done to him.

Keywords:

Egypt	minister	forgave
dreams	drought	

Questions

a. What was Yoosuf عَلَيْهِ السَّلَامْ well known for?

....

b. Why did the king call Yoosuf عَلَيْهِ السَّلَامْ from jail?

....

c. Why did the brothers of Yoosuf عَلَيْهِ السَّلَامْ come to Egypt? ....

d. How did Yoosuf عليْهِ السَّلَامْ treat his brothers?

....

e. Did Yoosuf عَلَيْهِ السَّلَامْ forgive his brothers?

....

Lesson eight

Yusuf عَلَيْهِ السَّلَامْ : Life in Egypt

Egypt

forgave

king

Colour in activity

Egypt

dreams

king

drought

forgave

minister

Lesson nine

Muhammad صَلَّى اللّٰهُ عَلَيْهِ وَسَلَّمْ - birth

1. Nabee Muhammad صَلَّى اللّٰهُ عَلَيْهِ وَسَلَّمْ was born in Makkah.
2. His father was Abdullaah, the son of Abdul Muttalib.
3. Aaminah was his mother.
4. Newborn babies of Makkah were sent to grow up in the farm areas where they were given special care.
5. Haleemah Saadia رَضِيَ اللّٰهُ عَنْهَا took Nabee صَلَّى اللّٰهُ عَلَيْهِ وَسَلَّمْ to the countryside, where she cared for him for four years.
6. Nabee صَلَّى اللّٰهُ عَلَيْهِ وَسَلَّمْ father Abdullaah had passed away before he was born.
7. Aaminah, the mother of Nabee صَلَّى اللّٰهُ عَلَيْهِ وَسَلَّمْ passed away when he was six years old.

Keywords:	Haleemah
Muhammad	Abdul Muttalib
Aaminah	Abdullaah

Questions

a. Where was our Nabee, Muhammad صَلَّى اللّٰهُ عَلَيْهِ وَسَلَّمْ born?

....

b. What was his father's name?

....

c. Who nursed Nabee صَلَّى اللّٰهُ عَلَيْهِ وَسَلَّمْ?

....

d. When did Abdullah, father of Nabee صَلَّى اللّٰهُ عَلَيْهِ وَسَلَّمْ pass away? ....

e. How old was Nabee صَلَّى اللّٰهُ عَلَيْهِ وَسَلَّمْ when his mother passed away? ....

Lesson nine

Sayyidina Muhammad صَلَّى اللّٰهُ عَلَيْهِ وَسَلَّمْ : Birth

Muhammad

Abdul

Muttalib

مُحَمَّد

Colour in activity

Muhammad

Aaminah

Haleema

Abdullah

Abdul Muttalib

Lesson ten

Nabee Muhammad صَلَّى اللّٰهُ عَلَيْهِ وَسَلَّمْ - childhood

1. Abdul Muttalib was the grandfather of Nabee صَلَّى اللّٰهُ عَلَيْهِ وَسَلَّمْ.
2. Abdul Muttalib took care of Nabee صَلَّى اللّٰهُ عَلَيْهِ وَسَلَّمْ after his mother, Aaminah passed away,
3. Nabee صَلَّى اللّٰهُ عَلَيْهِ وَسَلَّمْ was a very obedient child.
4. He never spoke lies or used bad language.
5. He was always very polite.
6. He did not fight or quarrel with his friends.
7. He was helpful in the house and also looked after sheep.
8. All those who came to know him loved him.

Keywords:

grandfather	polite
care	

Questions

a. Who cared for Nabee صَلَّى اللّٰهُ عَلَيْهِ وَسَلَّمْ after his mother passed away? ....

b. What type of a child was Nabee صَلَّى اللّٰهُ عَلَيْهِ وَسَلَّمْ?

....

c. Did Nabee صَلَّى اللّٰهُ عَلَيْهِ وَسَلَّمْ speak lies or use bad language? ....

d. How did Nabee صَلَّى اللّٰهُ عَلَيْهِ وَسَلَّمْ treat his friends?

....

e. During his childhood, what did Nabee صَلَّى اللّٰهُ عَلَيْهِ وَسَلَّمْ look after? ....

Lesson ten

Nabi Muhammad صَلَّى اللّٰهُ عَلَيْهِ وَسَلَّمْ : Childhood

grandfather

care

polite

Colour in activity

polite

grandfather

care

Lesson eleven

Nabee Muhammad صَلَّى اللّٰهُ عَلَيْهِ وَسَلَّمْ - character

1. From a very young age Nabee صَلَّى اللّٰهُ عَلَيْهِ وَسَلَّمْ showed special kindness to everyone, even animals.
2. He always shared what he had with other people.
3. He was helpful to the weak and the old.
4. The people of Makkah respected him for his honesty.
5. People also left their goods with him for safekeeping.
6. He was called Al-Ameen - The one who is trusted.

Keywords:

shared	Al-Ameen
honesty	respected

Questions

a. How did Nabee صَلَّى اللّٰهُ عَلَيْهِ وَسَلَّمْ treat animals?

....

b. How did he treat the weak and the old?

....

c. Why did the people of Makkah respect him?

....

d. Why did the people leave their goods with Nabee صَلَّى اللّٰهُ عَلَيْهِ وَسَلَّمْ. ....

e. What is the meaning of Al-ameen?

....

Lesson eleven

Nabi Muhammad صَلَّى اللّٰهُ عَلَيْهِ وَسَلَّمَ : Character

Al-Ameen

honesty

shared

respected